ALFA ROMEO
ALFETTA GT

Osprey AutoHistory

ALFA ROMEO ALFETTA GT

All 4-cylinder and V6 coupés

90243•EE

DAVID OWEN

Published in 1985 by Osprey Publishing Limited
12–14 Long Acre, London WC2E 9LP
Member company of the George Philip Group

Sole distributors for the USA

Osceola, Wisconsin 54020, USA

British Library Cataloguing in Publication Data

Owen, David,
    Alfa Romeo Alfetta GT: all 4-cylinder and
    V6 coupés.—(Osprey AutoHistory series)
    1. Alfetta automobile
    I. Title
    629.2′222   TL215.A3/
    ISBN 0-85045-620-7

Editor Tim Parker
Photography Mirco Decet

Filmset in Great Britain
Printed in England by BAS Printers, Over Wallop

Contents

Introduction

Two years ago, I wrote a book for the Osprey
AutoHistory series on the Alfa Giulia Spider – or the
Duetto – and its later, larger-engined descendants. In a
way, that was more than usually a labour of love, since
for nine years I had been the proud but demanding owner
of one of those splendid cars – and at the time of writing
the book, finding a worthy replacement for it was a
question which was very much on my mind. In the end,
given the car's pedigree, and its virtues, the most
sensible answer seemed to be to replace it with another
Alfa: but at that time, the Spider was no longer being
made in right-hand drive, nor was it being imported into
Britain. Given that a second-hand car wasn't the ideal
answer for the kind of driving, or the sheer amount of
driving, which I do as part of earning a living, there
seemed to be only one solution left. Alfa for years have
been renown for their open sports-cars – but for almost as
long a time, enthusiasts have delighted in their GT
coupés too. So the answer was to go for the latest in their
long line of closed cars – the Alfetta GTV. Despite some
misgivings – it was a decade and a half since I'd owned a
car with a roof on it – it proved to be every bit as wise a
decision as the original one had been to buy the Duetto
in 1967. And here at last is the final fruit of that decision:
the equally personal story of the GTV, what it was,
where it came from, what it could do, and how it is
developing into Alfa's new generation of models for the
later Eighties.

Once again, it's both a duty and a pleasure to record

the generous help given so freely by friends at Alfa Romeo, both in Italy and in England. In particular, Franco Perugia, Neil Verweij and Ray Corsi in Milan, and Barry Needham in London played their usual invaluable part in providing information and answering every kind of question. One can only hope that people who write books on other breeds of car can rely on the same kind of expert assistance. . . .

The family tree

It always seems slightly contradictory to begin a book on a particular model, or series of models, of car by delving back into the makers' history to long before the first lines of the design were drawn up on paper. Yet no car which has ever existed has been completely free of some influence from those designs which, successful or unsuccessful, took to the road before it. In some cases, the chassis was inherited from an earlier model, or it might share an engine with more familiar and already well-established stablemates. Or the links may be more tenuous: a particular layout, an individual configuration or perhaps a single philosophy may link the new design to others by different hands in a different country, at a completely different period in motoring history.

One of the factors which makes Alfa Romeo an interesting company to write about, is the policy of continuity in design which bridges the gaps between different models and even different generations since the company first began. In the case of the four-cylinder overhead-cam engine, still used for many of the company's current models, the story could be said to start with the original ALFA Grand Prix car of 1914 – at least so far as the basic engineering is concerned. And in the case of the car as a whole, the idea of a closed sporting saloon certainly dates back to the original GT coupés on the twin-cam 1500, 1750 and 1900 sixes of the late 1920s and early 1930s. But perhaps the best way to study the development of the GTVs of the 1970s

Contemporary shot of a classic 1930s Alfa Romeo 1750 with the superb Zagato body. These were the cars which inspired the whole of the postwar series of sports and GT cars. They were a pinnacle of traditional sports cars

and 1980s is to go right back to the beginning, and to pick out the different lines of the pedigree as they arise, and follow them through to the birth of the car which is the subject of this book.

At the very beginning of the Alfa story, the company wasn't even called by that name. It laboured under an entirely different quartet of initials – SAID – which actually stood for Societa Anonima Italiana Darracq, and was in fact a very early example of the well-known business practice of dumping. In other words, the already shrewd and successful Alexandre Darracq, who had made a sizeable fortune satisfying the needs of the progressively more demanding markets of France, Germany and Britain, was by 1906 looking for a less sophisticated set of customers on whom he could unload examples of his earlier models. The Italian market seemed to be ideal, since cars were still scarce, and roads fairly primitive, but enthusiasm and interest were present in plenty.

Unfortunately for SAID, this was one occasion when M. Darracq's normally reliable commercial judgment, seems to have failed him. Because of the harsh conditions of driving in turn-of-the-century Italy, and

Must be near to the end of a race at Donington Park in 1935 for the car is dirty and bits and pieces are hanging off. Type B Monoposto grand prix car, quickly known as the P3, was an Alfa Romeo tour de force *which further helped substantiate the company's sporting reputation. Could this be the Hon. Brian Lewis?*

because of the shrewd and discriminating knowledge of the would-be customers, the early Darracqs turned out to be precisely the cars which were *not* suited to Italian needs. So wide was the gap between what was offered and what was wanted, that the company was soon verging on bankruptcy. When, finally, it was rescued, it had changed its name to Anonima Lombarda Fabbrica Automobili, or Alfa. It had a different management – Alexandre Darracq having returned to the markets where his success had been founded – and, infinitely more important, a totally new range of models. Tough, reliable and dependable, they were an enormous improvement on the Darracqs, but as sporting vehicles, they seemed about as promising as an articulated lorry.

Yet the early Alfas were to prove remarkably effective in two respects. Toughness and reliability proved to be exactly what the customers wanted, and the steady sales of the 24 hp and 15 hp models put the company on to a sound commercial footing for the first time. Not only that, but once the heavy bodywork was stripped away, and the chassis narrowed and shortened, a racing version was produced which, while it might lack blistering acceleration or even out-and-out speed, still had the endurance and stamina needed to do well in the endurance epics of the day, like the Targa Florio. The 24 hp Corsa began the long story of Alfa's sporting success – it was soon succeeded by the larger and more powerful 40–60 Alfa, which did so well that within four years of restarting production after the reform of the company, the directors had decided to aim at motor sport's most difficult, and most expensive challenge, the domination of Grand Prix racing.

Even in the final years, before the First World War changed the face of Europe, GP racing presented a vastly different prospect from any other branch of the sport. No modified production vehicle, by the standards of the time, would stand a chance of delivering enough power and performance to keep up with the opposition – and reliability on its own would no longer be enough. So Giuseppe Merosi, the designer who had put Alfa on its feet in production terms, had to start again from the beginning with a much tougher set of requirements to meet than merely satisfying the needs of the car market. He had to design an engine which, within the capacity limits then operating, would work faster and more efficiently than others of similar size from more experienced and more lavishly supported competitors.

In the circumstances, it was a highly creditable effort. The engine embodied the best engineering practice, in that the side-valves of the production engine were replaced by two rows of inclined valves in the very roofs of the combustion chambers themselves – this cut down the distance to be travelled by the gases and the combustion products, in and out of the cylinders once the valves opened, to the absolute minimum. The combustion chambers were hemispherical in shape, so that the flame-front of combustion could sweep the whole space as quickly and efficiently as possible, to derive the maximum benefit from each charge of fuel-air mixture in the shortest possible time. Finally, to cut the inertia and complexity of the mechanism which opened and closed the valves as far as possible, each row of valves was actuated by a camshaft mounted directly above it. In summary then, hemispherical combustion

Prewar design, postwar racing. The type 158 with its 8-cylinder 1.5 litre supercharged engine was virtually unbeatable in the early postwar years. 'Alfetta' was their nickname

chambers, two rows of inclined valves and twin over-head camshafts – the standard prescription for the vast majority of Alfa engines ever since.

But the results were disappointing. The biggest problem with all the early cars was that they tended to be far too heavy for real performance, and in Grand Prix racing the standard weight-reduction programme was not nearly enough to make the car competitive. In fact, it had only just begun to show a glimmering of promise when the outbreak of war put paid to international motor sport for years to come. By the time peace returned, Alfa had fallen on hard times, and been taken over by successful entrepreneur Nicola Romeo, to be given its new identity as Alfa Romeo – and though the prewar car was brought out of retirement, it was clearly time for something new to take over the struggle for Grand Prix success.

Alfa Romeo's first attempt was a more ambitious design by Merosi, called the P1, which promised more than its predecessor, but which actually delivered less. It crashed on test before its first race, and killed works driver Ugo Sivocci, with the result that the team was withdrawn, and the company decided to cut its losses

and go for a more ambitious solution altogether. This was to use the good offices of two of its own employees, Luigi Bazzi and Enzo Ferrari, in persuading one of the top designers from Fiat's highly successful racing team, Vittorio Jano, to move to Milan to mastermind Alfa's racing efforts instead. The tactics worked, Jano switched employers, and set to work to produce a successor to the P1, with the logical but undramatic name of the Alfa Romeo P2.

In most respects, the engine followed what had come to be standard practice for Alfa, along with everyone else with aspirations to Grand Prix success: the twin overhead-camshafts, hemispherical combustion chambers and inclined overhead valves were the basis for a blown straight-eight which was fitted into a body which, at last, was light enough and strong enough to provide the right combination of performance and reliability. The rest is history: the cars began to win races from their first appearance in 1924, and the following season, in 1925, they won Alfa Romeo the company's first Grand Prix World Championship.

But in terms of the company's story as a whole, the real significance of Jano's success with the P2 was in

It's Reims and the 1951 Grand Prix of Europe with the type 159, essentially a modified 158. A long, apparently large car it was nearing the end of designs of this kind, to herald smaller and lower GP cars in the future. Handsome is as handsome does – it worked well

what was done with it afterwards. During most of the 1920s, the production cars had gone on as before, with size and solidity as major priorities, so that real performance had been at best an intermittent bonus. Merosi's series of push-rod overhead-valve fours and sixes, the RL and RM Normale, Sport and Super Sport had been large and imposing cars, but only the six-cylinder S and SS versions had possessed real sporting potential. When the time came to replace them, Jano took the exceedingly bold step of building a range of small, light and elegant six-cylinder cars around what was virtually the P2 engine with two of the cylinders, and the supercharger, taken away.

In true Alfa Romeo tradition, the production story of Jano's sixes, like most other models before and since, began quietly and sedately. The 6C 1500, as the original car was called, appeared in tourer, cabriolet and saloon form, and it proved to have immense appeal as a neat, inoffensive and stylish little vehicle. But the splendid engineering pedigree, of a production model which was actually based on a Grand Prix engine and chassis, apart from the use of a single row of vertical valves operated by a single overhead camshaft, was nowhere apparent to the average buyer.

Yet as time passed and more and more of the cars emerged from the Alfa Romeo workshops, newer and more ambitious versions began to make their appearance. The original 6C 1500 was replaced by a Sport version, which reverted to the double row of valves and twin overhead camshafts used in the racing cars, and featured a removable cylinder head of cast iron, instead of the fixed light-alloy head of the single-cam engine. This was followed in turn by the Super Sport (the names, and their sequence, suggested a similar process to the push rod RL models designed by Merosi which had appeared a few years earlier – though in this case the basic engineering was a great deal closer to racing practice than Merosi's cars had been). The Super Sport not only had the twin-cam engine, this time with a

Alfa's attempt at world class sports car racing after their retirement from grand prix racing in 1951 was not wholly successful although the cars showed promise. Fangio won the 1953 GP of Supercortemaggiore at Mercano only . . . the cars failed at Le Mans and Spa. Here's the coupé attempt. Although they were mighty cars perhaps their most memorable asset was their name, Disco Volante or flying saucer

The open car has more 'flaying saucer' about it than the closed version. In its day its looks were special. Note that it's right-hand drive. Its links with anything before or after are tenuous

15

CHAPTER ONE

In mid-flight of the production of the road going Alfetta GT, the Alfa factory were using grand prix racing again to promote their sporting product. Their changes in chassis and engine have been legion, as have their personnel and sponsors – this is 1979 with the name and badge written clearly

By 1985 things had changed this much and one might be excused for not knowing who has made the car. Their sponsors Benetton have endeavoured to use this connection in joint promotions, though. Meanwhile the Alfetta GT continues

higher compression ratio, but the chassis was shortened and lightened, a compact two-seat body was fitted, and the really enthusiastic buyer could order the optional Roots blower which really brought the car to life, with 76 bhp on tap from a 1.5 litre engine (real efficiency by the standards of the times) and a top speed of 87 mph.

By this time, Alfa's sporting efforts had turned on to a slightly different course. Having withdrawn from Grand Prix racing following the highly successful but ruinously expensive efforts in 1924 and 1925, the company had been dragged back to the track by the need to support the increasingly victorious efforts of a growing band of private owners, using tuned and modified versions of the RLSS and the sportier versions of the new 6C 1500s. In the end, Alfa took the most sensible action open to them: given that the efforts of the amateur entrants were keeping the firm's name associated with winning in the eyes of the public and, moreover, were doing it with cars which were recognizably the same as those sitting in the windows of everyone's local Alfa Romeo dealer, then providing a full-blooded works team to do to the job properly would still cost a fraction of the charges needed to return to the Grand Prix circuits. So they produced a strictly limited run of still faster and more powerful fixed-head engines for the works cars, with still higher compression and larger valves – these delivered 84 bhp from 1.5 litres and Campari and Ramponi proved only too well what the cars could do by driving one in the second Mille Miglia, the hotly contested marathon over a thousand miles of open Italian roads, and winning the event outright against the toughest possible competition.

Of course, there was no reason why the design, and its derivatives, should be limited to 1.5 litres, and it wasn't long before Jano and Alfa Romeo were following the apparently universal law that successful engines, like weeds and waistlines, just keep on growing. The bores were widened by 4 mm and the stroke lengthened by the same amount, to increase the capacity to 1752 cc. Although the standard version of the new model reverted to the single row of vertical valves and the single overhead camshaft of the 6C 1500, the Sport and Super Sport versions followed in rather quicker succession, and with higher performance figures to their credit. But there was one important difference, of particular importance to the story we're following in this book: the 1750 range was taken a whole step further, in that the Super Sport, with its optional supercharger, was followed by the Gransport with a supercharger as a standard fitting. And while the works two-seaters with the large-valve, fixed-head version of the engine, were capable of over 100 mph, even the production versions had power in plenty. So much power in fact, that a sports saloon version of the Gransport, with close-coupled bodywork, was capable of competing with out-and-out sports cars on virtually equal terms, with a top speed of 84 mph, but compact, closed-car comfort. It was called the 1750 Gran Turismo, and it was the ancestor of every GT car ever made, quite apart from its still more important role as the precursor of a brilliant range of Alfa sports coupés in its own right.

CHAPTER 2

The parents

Following the birth of the GT coupé, its descendants were to make regular appearances in the Alfa story up to the outbreak of World War 2. After the signal success of the 1750s, Jano set to work on something which was to be a great deal bigger, more expensive and more powerful – the straight-eight 2300. This used an ingenious modification of his P2 engine by virtually chopping the engine into two four-cylinder halves, which were then turned round and mounted back-to-back with the auxiliaries and camshaft drives in the centre, to reduce the length of camshafts and crankshaft and help to ensure strength and reliability. In fact, the car was a brilliant engineering and sporting success, but in the economic gloom of the early 1930s, it was a commercial disaster. The company had to be bailed out by the Government, and was forced to turn to less costly and less ambitious designs, which could sell in larger numbers, to ensure that it continued to survive in a time of shrinking markets.

All the same, the close-coupled, closed-bodywork GT coupé continued to play an important role in the company's affairs. The successor to the 8C 2300 was a much more mundane design altogether, on the surface at least. With a similar capacity of 2.3 litres to its eight-cylinder stablemate, its engine was actually based on a stretched version of the earlier six-cylinder design, and instead of a chassis frame of steel girders as on all earlier Alfas, it was based on a frame of welded steel box-sections, with saloon bodies of monumental proportions carrying seats for half a dozen passengers. But sporting customers were wooed by a short wheelbase version with a mere four seats and an 80 mph top speed called the Gran Turismo with closed bodywork by Alfa themselves, or by specialist coachbuilders like Farina and Castagna. Nor was the old competitive instinct quite dead: in the year of the new model's introduction, when Alfa were struggling to stave off closure, an extra-light four-seat closed coupé version, with bodywork by Carrozzeria Touring, was entered in the Targa Abruzzo, a 24–hour endurance race at Pescara. Three of the cars were entered, and they finished in first, second and third places. This particular closed coupé was known as the Pescara in commemoration of the victory, until one of its more streamlined successors won the Touring category of the 1937 Mille Miglia, taking fourth place overall, when the name was changed in honour of this still more remarkable victory.

In the final prewar years, Alfa's role in the Mussolini scheme of things was to, first, produce aero-engines for the escalating needs of the Italian Air Force and secondly, to outdo the teams of their German allies on the GP circuits of Europe. Car production came a poor third, and of the small number of vehicles which crept through the factory gates, a much higher percentage than before were closed sports coupés, with independent suspension, adjustable shock absorbers, synchromesh gearboxes and hydraulic brakes – streamlined and sophisticated models with a top speed of well over 100 mph, and cushioned luxury in a well-nigh irresistible combination for a fortunate few.

The Second World War proved to be an infinitely greater catastrophe for Italy than its predecessor had been a generation earlier. This time Italy was not only lined up among the vanquished rather than the victors, but its territory had been fought over and its cities and factories bombed. Alfa's own plant was so badly damaged by air raids that the only resource which was still intact was its own workforce. Machinery and

CHAPTER TWO

*Even the postwar 1900 could
provide a touch of the old
Alfa elegance: a 1953 coupé
by Castagna shows little sign
of its parentage*

*Another 1900: a lean 2 + 2
coupé by Farina with only the
front end revealing the car's
origins, pictured in the car
park at the 1953 Italian GP*

production facilities had to be painfully rebuilt, and
output had to be restarted, once the stocks of prewar
parts had been assembled into a stopgap production run,
with a new design which would be as modern, yet as
simple and as economical as possible.

The car which was to rebuild Alfa's postwar fortunes
was a plain, unassuming little saloon, with a four-
cylinder engine called the Alfa 1900. Many things had
changed with the passing of the war years: no
supercharger, no separate chassis, no luxurious interior,
no independent rear suspension, no sports version, no
flamboyant bodywork. Instead the car had a semi-
streamlined saloon body with four doors and a minimum
of decoration, a rigid rear axle which was, nevertheless,
carefully located to provide good roadholding and, most

importantly, an integral body-chassis combination which cut weight to the minimum but which made producing spider or coupé variants much more difficult and expensive.

There were some links with the past though: the cylinders were fewer, though they were still fed through two rows of inclined overhead valves in the roofs of the hemispherical combustion chambers, which were actuated by twin overhead camshafts as had been the case with Jano's prewar engines. And within a matter of months, the specialist coachbuilders had begun to work their usual conjuring trick, turning even the 1900's mass-produced monocoque into elegant, individual designs which were generally too expensive to appeal to more than the very favoured minority who could afford

The 2000 Sportiva, one of two experimental cars built around a bored out 1997 cc version of the 1900 engine. The idea of a limited production run for entries in the two-litre sports-car racing class, was never carried out

25

Carrozzeria Ghia produced two coupé versions on the Alfa 1900 series: this one, on the 1954 Super Sprint, was by far the more beautiful

A remarkable piece of prediction in sheet metal. The Touring design on the 1900 Super Sprint of the middle 1950s looks remarkably similar to the Bertone Giulia GTV of a decade later

Another stage in the progression: Bertone's first coupé version on the Alfa Giulia, the Giulia Sprint of 1964

premium prices. Even the relatively modest Touring-bodied cabriolet cost half as much again as the 1900 saloon, which was by no means a cheap car to begin with. And as far as Alfa itself was concerned, the choice was simple – the 1900 came in but one basic form, and options and additions were small, and few in number.

Yet though the 1900 had been designed with mass-production in mind, postwar regeneration progressed slowly, and the first cars had been virtually hand-assembled. All the special-bodied variants put together accounted for less than ten percent of the total of just over 21,000 cars made. Even by the middle 1950s, and the end of its run, output was still a long way short of target,

Rear view of the Sprint, a steeply-raked rear screen sweeping down to a small luggage boot. Sleek streamlining, but no room for rear-seat passengers

and only its successor, the immortal Giulietta, was to appear in the kind of numbers which made factory-built variants a real possibility. In fact, the first version of the Giulietta range to make its appearance, in the spring of 1954, was a completely new two-door coupé called the Giulietta Sprint, with two-plus-two accommodation and bodywork by Bertone, but offered from the start as a genuine Alfa model. The Giulietta saloon, which was the basis of the range and which was essentially a smaller, lighter and infinitely more beautiful version of the 1900, was to follow a year later.

Both the saloon and the Sprint coupé had the same engine, the small square 74 × 75 mm, 1290 cc version of

Above and right *Two
variations on the Alfa Romeo
closed coupé theme, both by
Bertone. The smaller, (above)
was the beautiful and
brilliant Sprint Speciale –
first on the Giulietta chassis,
and later on the Giulia. The
larger (right) was the 2000
coupé (later offered on the
2600) which used the bigger
car's dimensions to provide
room for four seats inside a
body shape which would later
be used on the smaller cars
with even greater success*

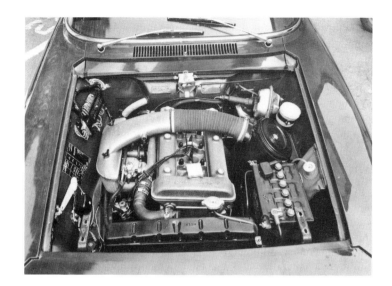

Both left *The Giulia Sprint coupé, with a revised roofline and two rear seats, became the Giulia Sprint GT (far left). Like all the others in the Giulia family, it was powered by a 1570 cc version of the classic Alfa twin-cam four-cylinder engine (left)*

the twin-cam four which had powered the 1900. In the saloon, with a compression ratio of 9.5:1 and a single downdraught carburettor, it delivered 53 bhp, which was enough to drive just over 2000 lb of motor car to a top speed of 86 mph. In the Sprint, the same engine with 8.5:1 compression, and a double-choke carburettor, produced 80 bhp and with a lighter body contributing to a total weight 77 lb lighter, had a top speed of 103 mph. But even more remarkable than the contrast in performance was the similarity in price – the Sprint was little more than a quarter as much again as the price of the basic saloon, and by the time the Giulietta range was superseded by the bigger and more powerful Giulia, no less than a quarter of the cars made were Sprints.

Clearly the combination of a sleek coupé body, four seats (even if the rear seats were less than luxurious), a more powerful engine, a higher top speed and a competitive price added up to a highly attractive car, and for thirty years since the first appearance of the Giulietta Sprint, Alfa Romeo have never been without a direct equivalent in their production model line-up. But the final ingredient in the winning formula was to take

CHAPTER TWO

*The uprated Giulia Sprint
GT became the Giulia GTV:
but the designation was
carried on to cover the coupé
version of the Giulia's
successors, like this 1750GTV
of the late 1960s*

another two years to arrive in full measure: the Sprint was a step in the right direction, but another stride towards greater performance was still needed – and in 1956, the Sprint's power output was notched up with an increase in compression ratio to 9.1:1, a second double-choke carburettor and a climb in power output to 90 bhp to produce the Giulietta Sprint Veloce, a 112 mph sports car with room for more than one passenger and a closed roof for protection from noise, draughts and bad weather.

When the Giulietta was replaced by the Giulia in 1962, the shape of the basic saloon was changed from the curves of the smaller car to the squared-off outline of the saloon version of the new 78 × 82 mm, 1570 cc range. But the two-seater open Spider which had joined the Giulietta range in 1955, soldiered on with the new engine as the Giulia Spider, as did the Sprint in its existing coupé form – to begin with at least. Gone was the 'Veloce' designation, as the new engine reverted to a single twin-choke carburettor, with 9:1 compression and

Alfa produced a series of smaller-engined versions of the Giulia models, to fill the gap left by the demise of the Giuliettas. This is the GT 1300 Junior, outwardly almost identical to the Giulia Sprint GT and GTV

92 bhp in standard form (only 2 bhp increase in power from a 20 per cent increase in capacity). But with body weight 20 lb heavier, the new car was actually 5 mph slower in top speed than its smaller predecessor.

This, however, was only a stopgap. And a year later, a stretched and refined version of the Bertone coupé with better aerodynamics emerged, with wider front track and clever reshaping which actually managed to provide more room in the back seats with a fractionally shorter wheelbase. This was the Giulia Sprint GT, which used a second twin-choke carburettor to help hoist the peak power to 106 bhp and, in spite of a weight increase to 2090 lb overall, managed to equal the top speed of the old Giulietta Sprint Veloce at last. And, perhaps most importantly of all, it sold for a lower price than the contemporary hotted-up saloon, the Giulia TI Super of fractionally zippier performance.

This slightly strange situation, where a prestige GT coupé was actually out-performed by an admittedly highly tuned version of its parent saloon model, was to persist for another three years, before the revival of the old 'Veloce' designation was to come to the rescue. The change was simple enough: a 109 bhp version of the Giulia 1570 cc twin-cam engine, which was still slightly

Far left *The final version of the first series of GTVs was the 2000GTV of 1970 onwards – an increasingly desirable collectors' property on today's market*

Above left *The driver's-eye-view of this GT 1300 Junior could stand for all the GTVs – wooden dash trim, large, boldly marked instruments and a beautifully direct gearchange and the unmistakably lively Alfa steering*

Above *And proof that the four-seater coupé concept really worked. The back seat access and accommodation on the GT 1300 Junior*

The GTV also had a vital part to play in Alfa's racing revival, from the GTA 1300 Junior shown here with 96 bhp, up to the supercharged GTA-SA which delivered more than 250 bhp

less powerful than that used in the Giulia TI Super in a body which was a couple of hundred pounds heavier, was still good enough – given good gearing and efficient aerodynamics – to equal its top speed of better than 115 mph. All in all, the GTV, as the Giulia Sprint GT Veloce was universally known to Alfa enthusiasts, was perhaps the most eagerly sought-after model in the range, for those who could afford the extra price. In just two years of production, more than fourteen thousand GTVs were made, and when the Giulia was replaced by the bigger and more luxurious 1750 range (by boring and stroking the engine to 80 × 88.5 mm and 1779 cc) the GTV appeared in the new line-up too. The 1750GTV was blessed with a twin double-choke carburettor installation and 118 bhp at peak, sufficient to boost top speed

to 120 mph, in spite of an all-up body weight of more than a ton.

The final step in the original GTV story was taken in 1972, after more than 44,000 of the 1750GTV had been made, which included 2475 of the special version made for the American market with indirect fuel injection to meet the emission requirements. This was brought about by boring the 1750 version of the twin-cam four out to 84 mm to raise the capacity to 1962 cc, the resulting model line-up being referred to as the 2000 range. The 2000GTV was actually lighter than its predecessor by 110 lbs, and with a peak power output of 132 bhp, the top speed was now as high as 123 mph, with brisk acceleration all the way up the range thanks to a splendid five-speed gearbox with the carefully spring-loaded lever which made for

The classic Alfa line-up of saloon, sports two-seater and GT coupé which has served the company for more than 30 years – in this case the 1600 cc Giulia Super and the Junior versions of the Spider and the GT . . .

delightfully fast changes, and the lively but sensitive steering which had long been an Alfa hallmark. Thanks to careful detail changes, the body design was still fresh after a decade of production, and more than 37,000 drivers were happy to opt for the combination of looks, comfort, space, performance and – surprisingly – economy, which the GTV had presented from the beginning. Not for the first time, it seemed that Alfa had stumbled across a real winner by a combination of chance and evolution rather than meticulous market research and deliberate design, and there was the very real chance that, as had happened before in different circumstances, they were too late to exploit their success to the full. It had already been decided that the 1900 chassis, through its reincarnations as the Giulietta, the Giulia, the 1750 and the 2000, was reaching the end of the road. What kind of car would replace it, and what chance was there of another GTV to keep the loyal customers happy?

CHAPTER 3

Alfetta GT

One fact which makes life difficult for historians trying
to trace the story of different Alfa Romeo model lines, on
a strictly chronological basis, is that for most of its life
the company has tended to overlap new models with
existing ones still moving out of the workshops, rather
than simply replacing one design which has reached the
end of its commercial life with a brand-new successor.
For this reason, it should come as no surprise that the
model which was to pave the way for the 2000GTV's
replacement was to make its own first appearance only
two years after the 2000GTV was introduced, while the
earlier model still had more than five years of production
still ahead of it.

Another enduring fact of Alfa Romeo life is that
design ideas which first evolved at a particular period in
the company's life to meet a particular set of requirements, often appeared again to meet similar needs
in an entirely different context. In the same way as
the twin-cam hemispherical-head four-cylinder engine
first appeared in the Grand Prix ALFA of 1914, later
emerged in an experimental 1.5 litre design of 1935 and
finally reappeared as the postwar saviour of the
company in the 1900 and its descendants, so other
aspects of design which had helped win the company
victories on the racing circuits were now to provide
improvements in the handling and behaviour of new
production models.

The start of this story goes back to the years before the
Second World War rather than the First. After Alfa

ALFETTA GT

The original Alfetta saloon of 1972: the simple and unassuming body-style hid a mechanical layout adventurous enough to merit the name

Three years later, and the original 1.8 litre Alfetta had been joined by a 1.6 version using the 1570 cc version of the twin-cam four – note the single pair of headlamps

Romeo had been taken under the wing of the Italian government, one of the company's new priorities had been to represent Fascist Italy on the Grand Prix racing circuits of the world. Looked at from one point of view, the task should have been simple enough: money no problem, a big staff of expert and professional engineers with little in the way of normal production problems to occupy their attention, and a solid heritage of sporting achievement on which to build. To many racing teams, struggling to triumph against far heavier odds, this kind of prescription must have seemed like a very unfair short-cut to success. Yet the results never matched the hopes of Alfa's own team, or their political backers.

Mainly, the reason lay in the fact that their main opposition came from another country with a similar prestige-hungry Government, an equal preoccupation with racing success, an even more generous attitude to financial backing, and an engineering experience every

The largest of the trio of Alfetta saloons, the 2000L, used the 1962 cc capacity version of the four-cylinder engine, and was fitted with rectangular headlamps and a more luxurious interior

bit as sophisticated: Nazi Germany. And where Alfa Romeo carried the Italian flag in the GP world virtually single-handed, Germany had two teams vying for ascendancy: Mercedes-Benz and Auto Union. The story of Grand Prix racing in the second half of the 1930s became a monotonous and dispiriting repetition of the same essential theme. Each new Alfa would outdo its predecessors in power and speed and acceleration, as the engines increased in complexity and sophistication from the classic straight eight to a V12 and finally a V16. But each time Italian hopes were given a new car to ride on, the German teams showed with almost contemptuous regularity that they were able to maintain their lead, and all too often the only question worth asking at the major circuits was – which German team would finish first?

The final prewar formula attempted to stop the rot by abandoning the all too free regulations which, by

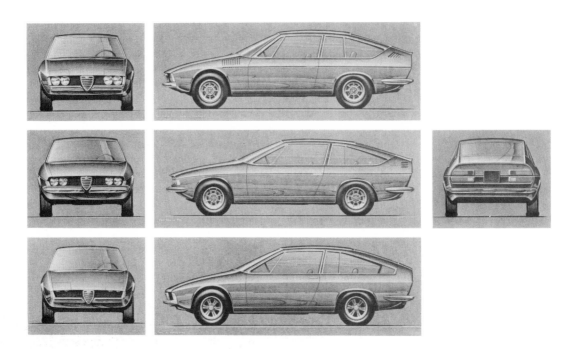

stipulating weight requirements rather than capacity limits, had left the doors wide open for an unbridled power race. The decision to standardize a maximum engine size of three litres should, in theory, have given all their major contenders an equal start, though it seemed no surprise that the German teams were once again either quicker off the mark in the other race, to develop a new contender, they were better prepared for the change.

For a nation as dedicated to motor racing as Italy, the situation was not to be borne lightly. Fortunately, there was one area of racing where international competition left them with a chance of victory. It had become practice to run races for smaller single-seater racing cars, called voiturettes, as curtain-raisers to the Grands Prix. While the GP cars proper were restricted to 3 litres, the voiturettes were limited to 1.5 litres, and were altogether cheaper and simpler – but the German teams

Left and above The Alfetta GT prototype takes shape: Giugiaro's original sketches (opposite page, top) show a variety of detail treatments, principally in terms of window shapes and, in the case of the bottom drawing, retractable headlamps. The middle sketch is closest to the design actually used. The lower pictures show the first full-size model taking shape. Even when it was virtually complete (above) the front door, window and windscreen pillar contours were still being revised, and the final design was closer to the version shown on the opposite page. The slots in the front wings didn't appear on the production car either

One of the pre-production prototypes (above) was sent to Stuttgart University for wind-tunnel tests. Other cars were submitted for crash tests: this one (right) showed only 560 mm of front-end collapse under some 20 g deceleration, which was a tribute to the strength of Giugiaro's design

didn't seem to be interested, seeing this less important class of racing as a distraction from their own priorities.

So the Alfa designers set to work to divert some of their resources into this much more promising area of competition. Their last prewar fling, so far as actual GP racing was concerned, was a three-litre V16 with twin superchargers which, though promising, still failed to deliver the combination of power and reliability in proportions which would present a real challenge to the German teams. But half of this engine would present a highly competitive 1.5 litre straight-eight, with a single supercharger which, fitted into a suitable chassis, could

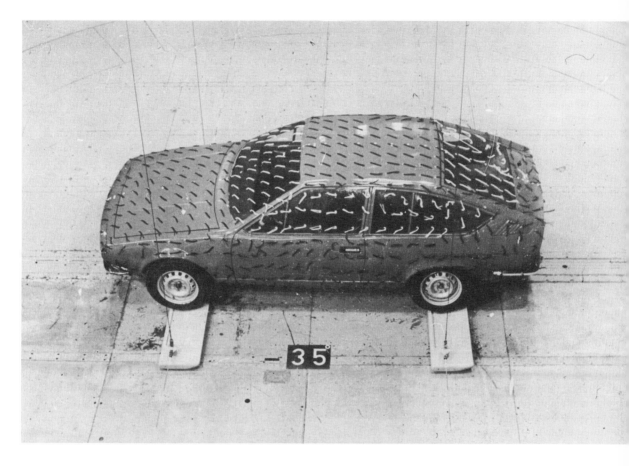

well dominate in voiturette racing and provide the loyal fans with some consolation for blighted national hopes.

Yet the engine was only half the problem. One of the reasons behind the crushing ascendancy of the German teams, in spite of the enormous increases in power produced by racing engines during the preceding years, was that they had designed and built chassis and suspension systems which could pour out the extra power on to the road without wasting it in wheelspin. Gone were the days when suspension design had simply meant harder and harder springing in an attempt to keep wheels in as close contact with the track as possible. The

Wind-tunnel testing in progress – in this case showing the airflow from a strong crosswind over the car body. Tests showed the production car body had a drag coefficient of only 0.39

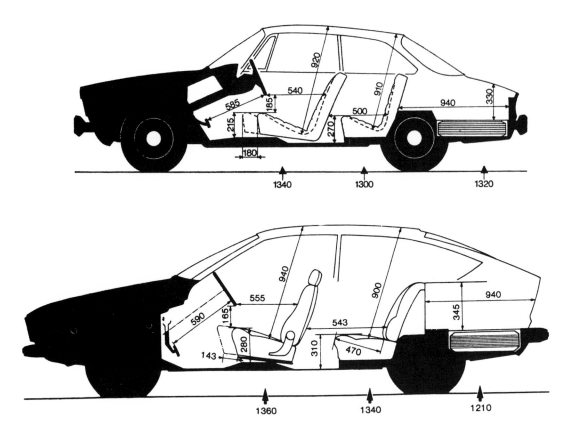

The acid test of Giugiaro's design was how it compared in terms of interior room with its well-loved predecessor. 2000GTV (above) has slightly more rear-seat headroom, but Alfetta GT (below) scores on front seat headroom, and legroom for back-seat passengers

new independent suspensions were proving to be vastly improved when designed and developed properly, but the main weakness was that a system which was less than the very best, could actually turn out to be worse than the old bone-shaking cart-springs and rigid-axle combination which had ruled the tracks for so long.

So Alfa paid a great deal of attention to the chassis of their new voiturette. Auto Union's success with rear-engined racing cars had thrown the problem of front-rear balance into sharp relief, and though Alfa were firmly committed to keeping the engine at the front of the car, they took the very bold step of placing more weight over the rear, driving wheels by shifting the clutch and the gearbox to the back of the car, in unit with the differential. On the original cars, the front and rear wheels were suspended independently by swing axles and transverse leaf springs, and with more than 200 bhp on tap, the little tipo 158 (the V16 GP car had been equivalent, as the tipo 316, to two 158s in the same chassis) was a very competitive contender indeed. Two cars came in first and second in the 1938 Ciano Cup on their first outing, and they triumphed again at Monza and Tripoli in the last season before the war.

But the finest hour for the little Alfettas came ten years later, when their 1.5 litre supercharged pedigree proved to be ideal for the new GP formula of the late 1940s and early 1950s. By this time the little cars were turning out almost 300 bhp, enough to propel them to a series of victories in the 1947 and 1948 seasons, and to the World Championship of 1950. Alfa won the title again in 1951, the uprated 425 bhp tipo 159 Alfettas, which had the rear suspension replaced by a more sophisticated and effective de Dion axle, to help make good use of the increased power delivered by the valiant little engine.

Following the second World Championship season, Alfa withdrew from racing, and the Alfetta name was retired to an honoured place in the history books. Until it appeared again two decades later, on a new production model which was both an exercise in nostalgia for past glories but also a genuine derivation of the original design to suit a new set of requirements, in the very best Alfa Romeo tradition. Essentially, the requirement was to find an eventual replacement for the popular but ageing Giulietta-Giulia design, which had itself evolved from the 1900 and which was now more than 20 years old.

There was clearly thought to be plenty of life in the engine, which had already appeared in 1290, 1570, 1779, 1884 and 1962 cc versions, with power output ranging from 53 bhp to 135 bhp (the racing versions took this figure up to more than 240 bhp with 11:1 compression and other detail changes). But the chassis was another matter altogether. At the time the 1900 made its first

A far cry from the hand-built bodies of prewar GT cars: the Alfetta GT assembly-line at Alfa's Arese factory in 1975

appearance, its lively yet predictable handling had been so far ahead of the field that Alfa had been able to stay with substantially the same design for a whole succession of otherwise new models. But in 20 years, the opposition had caught up – handling and roadholding had improved to the point where the Alfas were still holding their own, but were no longer unique in this respect.

Ironically enough, Alfa's own engineers, working on another project entirely, had shown what was possible with a clean sheet of paper and a team of open minds. The Alfasud, which was to make its first public appearance in the summer of 1972, seemed to be based on the ditching of as many cherished Alfa concepts as possible in a single design, with a flat-four engine, single camshafts, front-wheel-drive, McPherson strut front suspension with coil springs and a solid rear axle hung on a pair of modified Watts linkages. Although the car was designed as basic, cheap, mass-produced family transport, it turned out to have handling which put most of the sporting cars on the market deep in the shade – more embarrassingly for Alfa Romeo it showed up their own more traditional and more expensive models as being overdue for improvement.

So what could be done to regain their ascendancy, and put the competition in its proper place? Two areas for possible improvements offered themselves. Since the larger Alfas had stuck to the traditional front-engine, rear-drive configuration, the concentration of the majority of the car's weight over the front wheels was more of a problem than had been the case with front-drive designs like the Alfasud. Also the increasing popularity of more effective independent rear suspensions meant that the drawbacks of Alfa's rigid-axle layout were becoming more marked – what was needed was a further reduction in the unsprung weight at the rear wheels to enable the cars to handle well over poor surfaces or to respond well to rapid changes in steering demands without provoking roll oversteer. Another area where changes would be welcome would be in the eternal balance between handling and ride comfort. Alfas in the past had always shown a tendency towards rolling on entering a corner, though the ultimate roadholding had been good, provided the driver had the confidence to put up with large angles of heel – the softness of the suspension which produced this effect had allowed a comfortable ride, while the precise geometry of the suspension system had prevented things from coming unglued under the most severe cornering loads.

The first problem – ensuring even weight distribution between the front and rear of the car – had led many manufacturers to opt for the solution chosen by the makers of sports-racing cars. This meant mounting the

Another Alfa tradition was to introduce new models alongside their predecessors. These early production Alfetta GTs share the Arese production line with 2000GTVs, seen at the top right-hand corner of the picture

Final assembly of the first production Alfetta GTs at Arese

largest mass, made up by the engine-gearbox package, to a position as close as possible to the centre of the car, which in practice meant siting it just behind the driver and passenger. This solution was closed off to Alfa, however, since their tradition of practical four-seat sports saloons effectively limited the engine to one end of the car or the other. Yet the problem had been encountered 30 years before, by Alfa themselves, when they needed to replace the simple racing car suspensions of the late 1920s and early 1930s with something more efficient, to match the growing sophistication of the new designs of circuit cars. And the answer then had been embodied in the little Alfettas: to leave the engine where it was, at the front of the car, and to even up the weight distribution instead by shifting the rest of the power train to a position as close to the rear wheels as possible.

An idea which made good sense then, made equally good sense at the end of the 1960s. By shifting the clutch and the gearbox from their normal place behind the engine, and fitting them instead into a single light-alloy casting along with the differential at the rear end of the car, Alfa would be able to produce a chassis with ideal weight distribution, yet without disturbing the passenger compartment of the cars which used this chassis at all. There could be other advantages too, or so their thinking ran. By mounting this much larger differential casing directly on to the body-chassis unit of the car, just as had been done with the 1900 and its successors, the unsprung weight at the back end of the car could be kept as low as possible.

Nor was this all. Putting all this weight at the back of the car meant less weight on the front wheels, which opened up possibilities of revising the steering geometry to make use of this. The independent suspension on the Alfetta racing car had relied on swing axles and a transverse leaf spring, but now something much more sophisticated was needed. Alfa engineers opted for double wishbones, to eliminate troublesome camber changes under load. But the traditional coil springs were

replaced by long torsion bars, designed to provide a progressive-rate springing effect, so that the suspension setup could compensate for the effects of body roll under hard cornering without affecting the steering response.

The front suspension was entirely new: but the rear suspension once again put to use hard-won racing experience. When the postwar racing Alfettas had been made to deliver more and more power, the swing-axle rear suspension had proved totally unable to cope with the extra load, so Alfa's engineers had been compelled to redesign the rear end of the car. The answer in this case proved to be the de Dion axle, which though not a truly independent system had two very valuable advantages:

Alfa top brass show off their new model to President Leone at a special reception for the Head of State in May 1974

Side profile shows off angular shape of the windows and door. Cast alloy wheels are familiar 2000GTV options. Note shallow undernose spoiler

the de Dion tube ensured that the rear wheels were always kept upright and in line (which ensured predictable cornering with good roadholding) and the unsprung weight was actually limited to the weight of the simple tube linking the two rear wheels (which ensured a rapid response to bumps, uneven surfaces, or sudden movements of the steering wheel). But in going back to the racing know-how of 20 years before, Alfa were careful to take their usual care to guarantee adequate location, in this case by using a Watts parallelogram linkage with the central pivotal point fixed to the mid-point of the de Dion tube, and the ends of the two bars fitted to the mounting points of the suspension. This, and the use of coil springs to carry the body, helped limit the amount of sideways movement under load, all of which helped improve cornering performance.

Even though the engine of the new car was still the same well-proven twin-cam four which was hidden under the bonnets of the 1750s and the 2000s, this drive-train, chassis and suspension package added up to a

From the rear, the styling was undeniably successful in combining room for four occupants while still looking fast and elegant

formidable development problem. Designing such a radical configuration for racing cars which could be rebuilt – and often were – between one race and the next was one thing, but Alfa were contemplating making the same system, fitted to a mass-production car, stand up to the rigours and demands of tens of thousands of miles of everyday motoring. And before a single car could be sold to the waiting public, the engineers had to be sure that the inevitable teething troubles had been traced, identified, and eliminated, so that the new design could be made as rugged, reliable and dependable as the simpler and more orthodox 1900 had been, in a much less competitive world.

The omens were not good. Alfa's own engineers referred to the precedents of the original Lancia Flaminia, and a production Buick which had originally tried using a similar front-engine, rear-gearbox configuration but which had ultimately failed because of poor reliability. Porsche too had tried the same idea with the 924 and 928, and finally had to settle for a compromise with the gearbox remaining at the rear of the car, but the

Access to the rear seats (above left) was a lot easier than on earlier Alfa coupés . . .

But the dashboard (above, right) with its curious instrument layout, came in for plenty of criticism

clutch moving back to its more normal position behind the engine. And Alfa too found the problems were daunting: because the propeller shaft linking the engine to the rear transmission package was not turning at the same speed as the engine crankshaft (in a normal setup the propeller shaft is rotating at the speed of the output shaft from the gearbox, which is at a fraction of engine speed, depending on the gear ratio selected) the resonance problems reached undreamt-of proportions. On the early development cars, it seemed that propeller shafts and crankshafts were doing well to stand up to the battering vibrations for as long as 6000 miles before the fatigue shattered them to fragments.

Yet Alfa's policy of patient persistence paid off in the end. By splitting the propeller shaft into two shorter shafts, linked by three rubber couplings which helped damp out the worst of the resonances, they succeeded in taming the problems to the point where the new chassis design worked well enough to allow drivers to enjoy its advantages. But their job was far from over: another effect of moving the gearbox to the rear of the car was that the short, direct and very precise linkage which had made all Alfa gearboxes such a delight to use, was now replaced by a long and very tortuous arrangement indeed. Faced with a similar problem, by the use of a rear

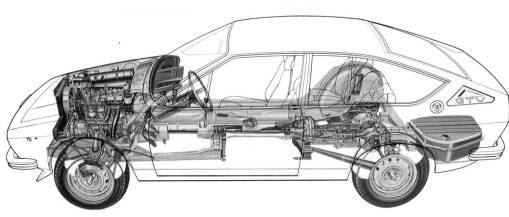

Above left *Lovely Alfa Romeo press shot of their launch Alfetta GT with the familiar 2000GTV cast alloy wheels. This car has fully white direction indicator lights – fit for which export market?*

Left *Alfetta GTV chassis ghost drawing. It readily shows off the rear axle mounted gearbox and forward clutch. A chassis to provide impeccable handling but often indifferent gear changing*

Above *The simple yet aerodynamically effective rear of the GTV (date 1976). Note the appropriate insignia/'air vent' which offers the quickest recognition point of this car*

Overleaf *The GTV comes of age with its 'second series' body styling. This is a 1980/81 GTV for the British market with the new style cast wheels and Pirelli P6 tyres, front spoiler and both front and rear bumpers*

Left *1979 and the Autodelta developed GTV 2.0 Turbodelta. The only external differences between this and the standard car, except for the paint, are those two vents on the bonnet*

Below *The factory went too far? This is a 1981 exercise in factory customizing known as the GTV 2.0 Grand Prix. Perhaps it's only the striping which doesn't work. Believed only to have been sold in Italy*

Above *Studio shot of a handsome silver GTV6 taken in 1983. Much more of the same! Those who love the classic Alfa twin-cam four, also love their excellent V6*

Right *Alfa interiors have long been known for their eccentricities. This GTV6, in fact, proves to be less so than the early Alfetta GT. Here, things are much more normal and familiar. Very much a car to be driven*

Far right *A 1983 model GTV6 photographed in England. The most popular colour still for any Alfa is their particular shade of red – metallic silver and black are not uncommon too. The overall shape remains dateless*

Above *1984 model GTV6 before the rain*

Right *Best known current Alfa Romeo driver in Britain has to be John Dooley; here in his GTV6 during a British saloon car championship round. His team is supported by Alfa dealers and Italian canned food company Napolina*

engine or a transversely-mounted front engine where a direct linkage to the gearbox was equally impossible, many manufacturers had opted for cables to link the gearlever to the gearbox selectors. The solution was cheap and simple, but anyone who has encountered the pudding-stirring feeling of moving a cable-operated gearlever around in the hope of finding *any* gear at all, would know only too well that the contrast between that and the old Alfa ideal would have been to much for the customers to bear. Losing a good gearchange for the privilege of better weight distribution and improved handling would have been like throwing the baby out with the bathwater. So the only alternative proved to be a mechanical set-up of rods and linkages which, while more complicated and more difficult to get to work easily and reliably, did at least offer some hope of a change which had the smoothness and precision of the old Alfa boxes.

Alfa's other problems with their new model, stemmed from these changes. Many potential buyers were traditionalists, who would need convincing that all these innovations really were genuine improvements. And any disappointments in a particular area would all too quickly blind drivers to the real if subtle improvements in areas like steering response and roadholding. So the decision was taken to market the new chassis in a single model at first, and to sell it alongside the still thriving 2000 range as a competitor rather than a replacement. But they had one trump card up their sleeve: to make the most of the radical features of the car's design, they could christen it after the car which had provided the inspiration in the first place. The decision was taken to name the new car the Alfetta, after its brilliant racing predecessor – and the company's hopes of an equally brilliant success on the commercial front were riding high when the Alfetta was shown to the press in May 1972.

Yet the beginnings were disappointing. As part of the marketing policy, the original Alfetta was a pleasant but scarcely exciting-looking four-door saloon which somehow lacked the panache of the boxy Giulia or the elegant curves of the Giulietta before it. It had the smaller and less powerful 1779 cc version of the twin-cam four, so that it was no giant in performance terms either. The moment of its appearance tended to be overshadowed by the launch of the equally radical and much cheaper Alfasud a month later, and its actual appearance in the showrooms was delayed for the best part of a year by a succession of industrial relations disputes which plagued Alfa's Arese plant for many months.

Only slowly did the world awaken to the Alfetta's virtues. Testers spoke of the improved comfort inside – though the wheelbase was shorter than the 2000's by two inches, rear seat passengers had the same amount of legroom and the interior of the car was actually wider by two inches. The smaller engine meant acceleration was down on the 2000, but the clean body style was more efficient aerodynamically, so that the Alfetta saloon boasted a useful 113 mph top speed, compared with the 120 mph of the 2000 saloon.

According to previous Alfa tradition, the appearance of the new Alfetta saloon should have been followed very closely by the entrance of a new sports coupé. But because of the low-key genesis of the new model, it was to be more than two years before this happened, by which time production of the saloon had finally got into full stride, and more than 65,000 had been produced, while the 2000 range was still happily soldiering on as if nothing had changed. Yet all the time development work on the Alfetta GT was proceeding apace, involving the same close collaboration between Alfa's own engineers and the Italdesign studio of Giorgetto Giugiaro – just as the Alfetta saloon had been entirely different in style from the 1750 and the 2000, to emphasize the different engineering design beneath the bodywork, so it was essential for the Alfetta GT to provide a complete breakaway from the familiar lines of the Giulietta, Giulia, 1750 and 2000 GT coupés. But would it be equally successful?

Giugiaro had been set an exceedingly tough assign-
ment. Alfa wanted to follow the precedent of the earlier
GT coupés by shortening the wheelbase of the saloon to
produce a lighter and more compact vehicle – in this
case, they called for a reduction of more than four
inches. The overall length was also to be three and a half
inches shorter, and the overall height four inches less
than the Alfetta saloon. The only increase was in the
width, increased by an inch and a half – but at the same
time Alfa insisted on providing adequate room for four
adults, and – more especially – minimum headroom in

the rear seats only an inch and three quarters less than the front seat headroom allowance. All this dictated a longer, flatter roofline than the sloping contours of the old Sprint GT and GTV coupés. This in turn, in the interests of good aerodynamics, suggested a high tail, which made possible a rear hatch rather than a conventional bootlid. So Giugiaro was able to draw the long sweeping curve which established the car as a genuine coupé rather than the rectangular outline of the three-box Alfetta saloon without compromising the rear-seat headroom by prolonging the sweep of the roof right back to the almost vertically chopped-off tail end of the car.

To balance the swept-up tail of the car, Giugiaro specified a low, sloping bonnet line, combined with a steeply-raked windscreen to provide a classic wedge shape, which produced good airflow characteristics. Early sketches showed one version with two pairs of retractable headlamps set into the top of the bonnet, but in most versions of the design, the lights were set in matched pairs in the front grille, and the only other changes embodied during the different stages of the design covered details like the bonnet contours, the shape of the windscreen pillars and the outline of the leading edge of the side windows.

Like all modern Alfa designs, the prototype was tested in full-size form in the wind-tunnel of the University of Stuttgart, and this resulted in some detail alterations, though others were apparently insisted on by Alfa themselves. Early sketches showed a flat bonnet with raised edges along the sides, though the final version had an almost completely flat bonnet lid, and Giugiaro's original intention to have the rear edge of the bonnet carried up to the base of the windscreen with the wipers concealed beneath the lip, in the interests of aerodynamic cleanliness, was rejected in the production car. The different cooling grilles and extractor outlets seen on the earlier designs disappeared on the production version, apart from triangular extractor outlets behind the rearmost corner of the side windows.

Other concessions to aerodynamics were unobtrusive – the rear edge of the tailgate was swept up into a very shallow spoiler to help the airflow leave the rear end of the car smoothly, and a chin spoiler beneath the front bumper was actually split into two parts, allowing a current of air to flow through the centre to cool the engine sump. The result was that the final design had a drag coefficient of 0.39, which was good by the standards of the time, and yet it still managed to look fast, and elegant, and – perhaps most important of all, given Alfa's

Left *The works rally cars of Andruet and Ballestrieri about to leave Genoa by sea for the Costa Brava Rally in March 1975*

Below *Ballestrieri's car in the scrutineering bay in the 1975 Costa Brava Rally*

Right *On the race-track too, the Alfetta GT proved itself a formidable contender. This is Klein's car in the 1976 Circuit of Mugello, a traditional Alfa event for half a century*

Far right *Klein again, this time leading a team-mate in the 1977 Spa 1000 Km*

marketing priorities at the time – entirely different from the preceding GT and GTV coupés. It was also a highly successful design in other respects too, as detailed torsion and bending tests of the prototypes showed that it was actually stiffer than the body of the Alfetta saloon, though the actual reduction in weight was only of the order of 22 lb.

The result was that when the car made its first public appearance in June 1974, most commentators seemed happier with the external design than they did with the interior. Having gone to the trouble of fitting an opening tailgate, which was supported by a single gas-filled strut, and which was connected to a lifting inner lid which gave access to the boot proper, it seemed strange Alfa had not taken the logical next step and offered buyers the best of both worlds. Providing genuine access to the rear seats, and contriving an arrangement for the rear seats to fold, would have dramatically increased the versatility of the car. As things were, the boot space was good by coupé standards, but the high sill made loading and unloading of heavy objects quite difficult.

But perhaps the most controversial feature of the original Alfetta GT coupé, from the driver's point of view, was the unusual instrument layout. Although the basic driving position was comfortable enough, for shorter drivers at least (the usual Italian blind-spot

regarding taller drivers was undeniably present, offering the usual choice between hunched-up knees and outstretched arms), with well-shaped seats and a steering wheel which was adjustable for height, the only dial which the driver could see in his direct line of sight behind that wheel was a rev-counter. The other instruments – the speedometer, the fuel-gauge, the oil pressure gauge and the water temperature gauge – all resided in a panel in the centre of the dashboard which meant a real distraction of attention from the road to check their readings.

Alfa's explanation for this idea seemed to lack a sense of reality. The argument that the rev-counter is the most important instrument of all is one which few drivers would quarrel with on a racing car, where maximum performance and the most efficient timing of gear-changes are the major priorities. But in ordinary road driving, particularly where speed limits and not actual road conditions dictate the maximum reasonable speed, the speedometer becomes paramount, and it came as little surprise when the right-hand-drive versions of the Alfetta GT which appeared on the British market had these instruments transposed.

Other details of the design gave the impression of being attempts to solve inherent problems. Because of the lower roofline, some drivers found the headroom restricted: those who didn't, were able to use the driver's seat height adjustment (an ingenious pull-out crank handle on the side of the seat itself) to raise themselves up to provide a better view forward over the bonnet. Through ventilation was adequate, but in hot weather it was essential to lower the rear side windows using the cranks provided for rear-seat passengers – but the body contours only allowed them to be partially lowered at best. A catch at the side of the front seats allowed the seatback to be folded forwards, and a linkage ensured that the seat itself moved forward bodily when this was done, to improve the otherwise very restricted entry to the back seats. Yet there were two genuine improve-

The might-have-been in the Alfetta stable – a Pininfarina design for a spider on the Alfetta chassis

ments over the saloon: a larger fuel tank and wider-section tyres to improve range and roadholding.

The press reaction to the new car was a qualified welcome. *Autocar* referred to the 'new and pretty body, in this case by Giugiaro himself' and went on to praise the aerodynamic efficiency 'backed up up by a set of impressive steady-speed fuel consumption results: 46.7 mpg at 40 mph, 35.8 mpg at 60 mph, 26.4 mpg at 80 mph and 20.1 mpg at 100 mph'. They noted that the car had not been given any extra tuning over and above the Alfetta saloon (this trend had already become established with the 2000 saloon and 2000GTV), but quoted Alfa's rather unexpected explanation. Apart from extra power not being considered necessary, Alfa spokesmen referred to a recently-introduced Italian regulation

The Pininfarina Spider would have made an all-Alfetta line-up, with the saloon and the Alfetta GT, of Alfa's three traditional variations on a theme. But the model never went into production, and the open-top customers are still catered for by the Giulia-based Spider 2000

which prohibited drivers under 21 or over 65 from driving cars whose homologated top speed was higher than 180 km/h. And, it seemed, the top speed of the Alfetta GT was – exactly – 179.5 km/h, or 112 mph.

What mattered, though, was how the car reached this speed, and how it behaved when it got there. And in these respects, testers awarded it high marks indeed. *Autocar* found it '. . . in every way respectable for a four-cylinder GT coupé of well under 2 litres, and . . . only disappointing if one is looking for a notable improvement over the saloon. In some ways, the GT feels quicker, mainly because it is rather noisier – one suspects almost deliberately so'. On the other hand, the gear ratios were very well matched to the power output of the engine, and the handling was rated as well-balanced and free from vices or unexpected surprises. Some testers found the ride on the harsh side, others felt it was softer and prone to initial roll in the traditional Alfa manner on entering a bend, though the car stayed on line with few problems through the corner itself.

The only problems revealed on the first driving-impression outing with the car in Italy, apart from the instrument layout which everyone found unusual if not downright confusing, was the tendency of the steeply-raked windscreen to reflect all the instruments and warning lights in the driver's line-of-sight, and the way in which the inside of the car reached uncomfortably high temperatures on a sunny day due to the greenhouse effect of the glass. The ventilation system definitely found difficulty in coping with this, unless one or other of the rear side windows was opened, and the car was kept moving. But operating the window catch from the driving seat (if no-one was sitting at the back to undertake the job) was an ideal prescription for all kinds of troubles from slipped discs to double hernias if undertaken carelessly.

Having said all this, every car ever made is a compromise, a combination between good qualities and the inevitable small drawbacks which can often obscure the positive advantages of the design, because of the way in which they can irritate or distract the driver from an objective appraisal of the car. And the Alfetta GT had certain undeniable advantages: it was a superbly balanced machine in three different respects. Its looks were a careful balance between the needs of aerodynamics on the one hand and practical passenger and luggage accommodation on the other. Its engineering was not only a virtually ideal balance between front and rear in terms of weight distribution, but also a clever compromise between traditional and well-proven ideas and genuine and worthwhile innovations. And as enthusiasts had come to expect from Alfas over the decades, the complete package was a careful balance between the power delivered by the engine, the gear ratios, the suspension settings, the four-wheel disc brakes (outboard at the front, inboard at the back), the steering geometry and the tyre characteristics.

This was really just as well, since at the time the Alfetta GT was introduced, it was very slightly slower up the acceleration curve than the 1750GTV, and it was actually up against that car's successor, the 2000GTV, with 10 more brakehorsepower on tap, in Alfa's own model line-up. So its improved handling and greater comfort, not to mention its up-to-the-minute looks were of paramount importance in guaranteeing its commercial future. Even so, sales were slow to start, and it was a full year before the first Alfetta GTs reached the British market in any numbers, while another year would see its replacement by not one, but two, new versions.

CHAPTER 4

Return of the GTV

The summer of 1976 produced the first step in the development of the Alfetta GT, with the original 1.8 litre engine version being replaced by two outwardly identical successors, one with a smaller version of the twin-cam four, and one with a larger. After more than a quarter of a century with essentially the same engine in a series of different sizes and measurements, this exercise might have been nothing more than a return to the parts bin for Alfa Romeo, to pick out a different set of bits and pieces to produce the characteristics they wanted. But in actuality, it was a careful and painstaking process which was designed to maximize the GT's appeal in the market-place.

Whatever the truth of Alfa's explanation, as quoted by *Autocar*, that the reason why the original Alfetta GT had not been given any extra power over and above its saloon parent had been the introduction of a law forbidding drivers under 21 and over 65 from taking the wheel of a vehicle whose designated top speed was more than 180 km/h, the smaller of the two new variants had stayed within this limit. But it had done so with a smaller engine than the 80 mm bore, 88.5 mm stroke, 1779 cc version fitted to the original GT. In fact, it returned to the 78 mm bore, 82 mm stroke, 1570 cc version of the twin-cam four which had powered the Giulia range, and in particular to the kind of tune which had been used for its ancestor, the Giulia Sprint GT Veloce coupé of 1966. This had 9:1 compression, two horizontal twin-choke carburettors (though they were now Dell'Orto rather than Webers) and delivered a peak power of 109 bhp, though at a slightly more leisurely 5600 rpm than the 6000 rpm of the old GTV. Other modifications included considerably larger valves: 41 mm inlet valves, compared with the 37 mm valves of the Giulia GTV and the 38 mm valves of the Alfetta GT 1.8 and 37 mm exhaust valves instead of the 31 mm valves fitted to the two earlier cars. At the same time, the rear axle ratio was increased to help improve the overall performance – the

Outwardly little different from the 1.8 litre Alfetta GT, the Alfetta GTV had the 1962 cc version of the twin-cam four-cylinder engine

Right *Heart of the Alfetta design – and the ultimate justification for the name – was the rear-mounted clutch-gearbox-transaxle assembly, and the de Dion rear suspension*

Below *Spot the difference – the rubber over-riders, chrome strips in the front grille and the 'GTV' motif in the rear extractor louvres, stamp this car as the Alfetta GTV 2000 rather than the original 1.8 litre GT*

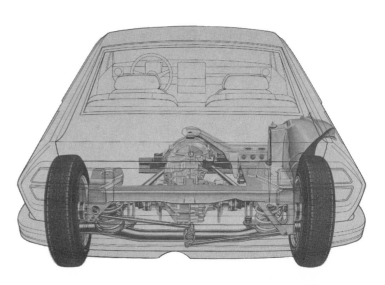

original GTV had had a lazier rear-axle ratio but the earlier five-speed box had busier ratios at the top end than the all-indirect five-speed box used on the Alfettas. Outwardly, in all other respects, the car was identical with the original 1779 cc Alfetta GT – but it was officially designated the Alfetta GT 1.6.

Its stablemate, introduced at the same press showing in May 1976 in Florence was a larger engined version of the original car which, logically enough, used the 84 mm bore, 88.5 mm stroke, 1962 cc version of the Alfa twin-cam engine as used in the 2000GTV, but with larger valves – this time inlet valves of 44 mm diameter were fitted, with 40 mm exhaust valves – and, strangely enough, no increase in overall power over the 1.8 engine, except that the 122 bhp power peak was reached at a lower engine speed of 5300 rpm rather than 5500 rpm. Because of this, the lazier 10/41 rear axle ratio (the GT 1.6 had a 10/43 ratio) of the original Alfetta GT was retained, but because of the engine's beefier torque characteristics, the car's performance improved quite markedly, with a top speed of 120 mph and just over a second cut from the nought-to-sixty miles an hour time from a standing start. So although there was no increase in power to justify the term, the increase in speed made a good case for the revival of another of Alfa's revered titles from the past: and the two-litre version of the Alfetta GT coupé became, almost inevitably, the Alfetta GTV2000.

These two cars were to have very different commercial histories. At the time of their launch, the 2000GTV still had a year of production to run, and in fact the Alfetta GT 1.6 only stayed in production itself for four years, during which time it was a moderate success. But the real best-seller, in coupé terms at least, was the GTV, which at the time of writing is still part of Alfa's current model line-up, and which from the very beginning outsold its smaller-engined sister by a ratio of between two and three to one.

And here at last, I can inject a personal note into the

Overleaf Just as with the earlier GTs and GTVs, there was little to mark the · increased power in the new 2-litre Alfetta coupe, in terms of external embellishments

91

Because of the American market's unfamiliarity with the Alfetta legend, the models were sold on the other side of the Atlantic under slightly different names. The saloon became simply the Alfa Romeo Sport Sedan, and the GTV became the Sprint Veloce

story. Following my long and happy relationship with my Alfa Duetto (see *Alfa Romeo Spiders* in the Osprey AutoHistory series) which was abruptly terminated in January 1976 following a spectacular but ultimately terminal electrical fire, I had long been on the lookout for a replacement Alfa until, three years later, I decided to bow to the inevitable and accept, for the first time in 16 years, the inevitability of closed-top driving. At the time, the Alfetta GT 1.6 was on sale in Britain at around a thousand pounds less than the Alfetta GTV, and the price differential seemed too large to ignore. I tried to place an order, but without success, as I was told the model was being phased out on the British market (this was early in 1979) leaving only the two-litre car.

It was a decision to agonize over, made worse by the fact that a colleague had been able to buy one of the last right-hand-drive 1.6s, which he had enjoyed very much,

but had found that his wife felt the lack of headroom quite claustrophobic. He traded the car in, after only a few weeks of ownership, for a Giulietta 1.6, and the option of a nearly new, second-hand Alfetta GT was a tempting one. In the end, the colour (it was white) was decisive – apart from a firm conviction that Alfas ought to be made in Italian racing red, I'd had some unfortunate experiences with the rust-proneness of white-painted cars, which eventually tilted the scales. And a chance to road-test the Alfetta GTV, as part of the research for an earlier book on Alfa Romeos (*Alfissimo* – Osprey Publishing) was effective in settling the matter. Driving the car back to London on a clear, cold day in early spring, another driver pulled out of a side road without warning – a truck was coming the other way, and a touch on the brakes revealed all too clearly an unexpected patch of black ice. The only option left was

The SE version of the GTV, at least in Britain, featured an uprated specification which included features like a sunroof, electric windows and special lamps and roadwheels

to leave the brakes alone and steer round the obstacle, which the perfect balance of the GTV made a simple business, even on a road surface about as helpful as polished steel for manoeuvres of any kind. After that, I was hooked – a GTV it had to be.

So it was, I took delivery of a red Alfetta GTV2000 from Alfa Romeo's London Edgware Road headquarters at the beginning of August 1979. The drive back home was a joy, with the combination of Alfa steering, Alfa handling and Alfa noises after an absence of more than three years. The only untoward symptom was a slight but definite rumble from the front end of the car whenever it went round a right-hand bend. The next day, there was time to investigate – it turned out the fixing nuts on the front nearside wheel were barely finger-tight. . . .

Yet that was the only really worrying fault in four years of ownership, during which the car and I covered the best part of 80,000 miles in one another's company. True, we didn't range as far and wide as I had done with the Duetto, but the car proved to be even more reliable than the earlier one had been. Like its predecessor, it refused to go but once in all that time, and in this case the trouble was both simpler and cheaper to cure – a failed battery rather than a useless water-pump. Apart from that, it lacked the earlier car's appetite for exhaust valves (perhaps the larger valves helped here) and the only irritations were a collapsed parcels tray and a loose fresh-air vent which persistently refused to stay in place for long.

The car was always delightful to drive. Although there had been a lot of controversy in the motoring press during the two years before taking delivery, about the alarming variations in behaviour and build quality between individual cars in the Alfetta-based range, (specifically Giuliettas, though some of the Alfetta GTs came in for criticism on the grounds of sub-standard shock absorbers, badly set-up suspensions and quirky gearchanges) all fears proved totally groundless. The

The GTV Strada, available only on the British market, was fitted with extras like cast-alloy wheels, an electrically-operated sunroof and windows, and extra lights

gearchange did, undoubtedly, lack the splendid direct-
ness of the old front-mounted Alfa box, but it was very
rare that one hit the wrong ratio by mistake. The careful
Alfa spring assistance made downshifts quick and easy,
though there was an extra fraction-of-a-second pause
compared with the old box, while the linkages took the
demands of the driver's left hand and translated them to
actions at the opposite end of the car.

Some critics have mentioned the noisiness of the
Alfetta GT coupés compared with the equivalent
saloons, but the noise level in my GTV was never
obtrusive. Others claimed that the steering was dead,
and that the marvellous lively feel of the old coil-spring
front suspension in models like the Giulia, had been lost
for ever – again, I didn't find it so. It's difficult to point to
precise illustrations of handling improvements resulting
from the better weight distribution, though in one

*Opposite and above The 1980
version of the GTV – not only
bigger and stronger front and
rear bumpers, revised wheels
and trim, but the '2.0' in the
nameplate indicating the
appearance of the more
powerful four-cylinder GTV*

respect the GTV left the distinctly nose-heavy Duetto standing. When there was snow on the ground, and traction was at a premium, there were cases when the Duetto's rear wheels couldn't find any grip at all. But unless conditions were absolutely impossible, the GTV would usually do as it was asked – until one occasion when it met a Volvo estate coming too fast around a blind bend in the snow. The GTV stopped quickly, impeccably, without fuss. The Volvo locked its wheels and slid into a head-on thump, writing off the GTV's front bumper and bending the panelling.

As a motorway cruiser, the GTV wasn't the best in the world. At times, one was too conscious of engine noise to push the car to its limits, when much more mundane vehicles would be pushing past in the fast lane. But the conditions where the car came into its own were the kind of long, cross-country trips over winding roads where traffic was light, but car and driver had to work hard to keep up any kind of sensible average speed. Then the

ever-willing engine, the even spread of ratios in the gearbox and the splendid handling really came into their own: the driver has almost a choice of handling characteristics, depending on how well he knows a corner and how he approaches it. Leave the turn into the corner late, and apply the steering too sharply, and the car would tend to understeer: on the other hand, easing the car into the corner and pouring on the loud pedal would provoke a measure of oversteer. But time the corner properly, and enter on the correct line and the car would do almost anything asked of it, staying perfectly neutral and balanced up to the point where it would begin to scrub sideways on all four wheels, but always progressively and controllably, and only at the highest cornering speeds. There seemed to be literally no surprises at all. Even the classic error of entering a corner too fast, and lifting off abruptly in sheer panic,

Four years on, and the chrome has all but disappeared, along with the 'GTV' on the rear quarters

produced a tendency for the car to tighten its line through the corner, just as the Mini had done with entirely different drive and weight distribution arrangements, under the same circumstances.

There were several worthwhile ideas which ownership of the car enabled one to value at their true worth. Having the fusebox inside the car, with its own lid and light, just to the right of the steering wheel, was so much more convenient than having to get out and hunt for it under the bonnet, possibly in driving rain or freezing darkness. The hefty footrest for the left foot is an important aid to comfort on long-distance runs, particularly since the movement needed to transfer the foot to the clutch pedal is an easy and natural one. The wind-down rear windows transformed the warm-weather ventilation inside the car, though on the GTV the original winding handles had been replaced by circular grips which had to be rotated rather like turning a tap – trying to do this at full stretch from the front seat was even more of a problem than before.

Visibility was never really a problem. It was impossible not to be aware of the reflection of the instruments in the screen at night, and a digital clock which was fitted as an extra could actually be read by its screen image, provided the figures were reversed – without taking the eyes off the road, it worked as a primitive and unintentional form of HUD (head-up-display) of the kind now fitted to low-flying combat aircraft. But the four-headlamp combination threw a superb beam of light which lit up the road for an enormous distance ahead, so reflections never really proved a distraction. In fact, the only problem with the lighting was that unless the lenses were kept really clean, the two headlamps available on dipped beam were so dim compared with the full quartet that one felt temporarily blinded until able to switch back to full beam again.

Daytime visibility should have been clear enough, thanks to the thin windscreen pillars, but there were

Left, right and below *A big power boost for the classic Alfa 2-litre engine thanks to a turbocharger fitted by Autodelta (right). This engine was used in the Alfetta GTV 2.0 Turbodelta competition car*

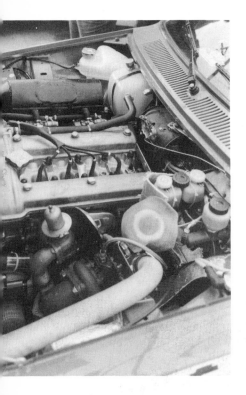

Above *Autodelta's Group 4 turbocharged GTV, at the Costa Brava Rally*

In its final competition form, the Turbodelta GTV was a formidable beast indeed, festooned with lamps and crowned with air scoops to keep the engine breathing hard

More fearsome still was the Alfetta GT V8, which used a modified version of the engine developed for the Alfa 33 sports racing cars to run in Group 5 events

sometimes problems when the combination of a narrow strip of screen left unswept by the wipers and the steep rake of the pillars themselves, did sometimes obscure the view of traffic coming from one side or the other – and the rear quarters could make life difficult when filtering on to a motorway. That apart, the car's only other defects were a certain appetite for exhaust pipes, and the near impossibility of cleaning the extractor vents behind the rear side windows, as the simple louvres of the Alfetta GTs had been replaced by a stylized 'GTV' which proved a perfect trap for soap, water and the corners of washleathers.

There is another point which has to be borne in mind, when placing the Alfetta GTs in their context. The initial model appeared at the beginning of another very difficult period in Alfa Romeo history, and the GT 1.6

The Alfetta GT V8, covered in air scoops and ducts for brake cooling, running in the Valli Piacentine Rally, driven by Ballestrieri

and GTV2000 were launched when the company was facing daunting challenges from a number of different quarters. One problem was the struggle to establish the Alfasud operation in Naples, and bring production up to the point where the company could actually meet the unexpected demand which had arisen for this highly desirable little car. Another was the onslaught on Alfa's traditional markets from Japan, and from increasing competition within Europe, which was hitting sales of the company's established models very hard indeed. Thirdly, increasing industrial unrest within Italy had delayed the original Alfetta saloon, and was to cause persistent quality control difficulties with other models in the company's range, among them the Alfetta GT coupés. Finally, had these not been enough on their own, changes in the composition of both the steel supplied to

Right and below *In England, Alfa dealers Bell and Colvill of East Horsley, offered a roadgoing turbocharged GTV, using a Garrett AiResearch blower*

car makers (which used more reconstituted steel in an effort to cut costs) and of the road salts used all over Europe to treat roads in winter, combined to produce formidable challenges to existing rustproofing measures. Alfa themselves had gone through a bad period with rust problems during the 1960s, and now it seemed, it was happening all over again.

Yet improvements had been made, and a direct personal comparison between corrosion on my 1967 Duetto with the 1979 GTV shows how much the company had achieved in that time. Underseal protection was more obvious and more effective, and though localized patches of damage to the paintwork were initiated by stone chippings thrown up by other vehicles, keeping the bodywork in good condition was a great deal less of a chore than it had been. The areas which suffered most were those around the lower parts of the doors and the curved undertray of the body, where mud and gravel were flung up against the paintwork, and it's noticeable that today's Alfas have noticeably thicker protective coatings over these vulnerable parts of the cars.

Alfa also went on to greater lengths to capitalize on the comfort of the car by offering various optional extras, and in January 1978 they put together some of the most desirable extras in a Strada version which was unique to the British market and was originally to be produced in a limited edition of three hundred examples. Costing £6898 at the time of its introduction, it included as standard features electric windows, an electrically operated sunroof, a power-operated radio aerial, light alloy wheels, velvet upholstery and headlining, Hella foglamps front and rear, and a Blaupunkt stereo system.

Yet for a large part of the GTV's life, perhaps the biggest disappointment for Alfa enthusiasts was that the splendid chassis was not given an engine which was powerful enough to use its handling to the limits. Surrey Alfa agents Bell & Colvill went some way towards remedying this in the late Seventies, when Alfa announced that they would not be making the Autodelta-developed turbocharged version of the GTV, already on sale in the German market, available in Britain. Bell & Colvill had produced their own turbo Lotus Esprit, and they felt the GTV offered ideal material for a similarly careful treatment. In fact the engine itself, with its sodium-cooled valves, needed very little changing beyond the fitting of Cosworth forged pistons to provide a lower 7.2:1 compression ratio and to cope with the extra heat generated by the turbocharged engine. The exhaust manifold also had to be replaced by one made from special heat-resistant steel, and the brake servo had to be moved from the exhaust side of the engine to the inlet side, where it could be kept cooler. (Since right-hand-drive cars had to have a cross-shaft to connect the brake pedal to the servo on the left-hand-side of the car, this actually made for a neater arrangement.) Higher oil temperatures were kept in check by fitting an oil cooler, but the major change was the addition of a Garrett AiResearch turbocharger, blowing at up to 7 lbs pressure through the car's twin Dell'Orto carburettors, and lifting the power to a new peak of 175 bhp at 5500 rpm.

The effect on the car was dramatic – smooth acceleration all the way up the range, with 60 miles an hour coming up in only eight seconds from a standing start, or a full second and a half faster than the standard car. In another 14 seconds, the turbo car would be travelling at 100 mph, while the standard GTV would be approaching 85. Because the gearbox and rear axle ratio were unchanged, the turbo car's top speed was limited by engine speed rather than the power available, but 125 mph was a comfortable top speed which could be reached quickly, and with ease. I drove one of these cars at the time when I had my own GTV for a direct comparison, and in all respects save acceleration, the cars seemed identical: noise level, flexibility, handling were equally good in both. As with many turbo cars, they even seemed the same lower down the speed range, but once the revs began to climb, the expected tailing off of performance before the next gearchange seemed to take forever with the turbo, with the speed climbing smoothly and inexorably in the meantime. Even the fuel consumption was a good deal less than horrific – my GTV averaged 27 mpg over its life, and the turbo averaged just over 24. That – and a purchase price of £9995 – were the only penalties, and the only thing which blighted the car's real promise was the action taken by Alfa themselves to provide the same extra performance in a different way, as we shall see in the next chapter.

CHAPTER 5

The GTV6

For most of the story of Alfa Romeo since the war, let alone that of the Alfetta model range, one factor at least has been constant. The splendid all-alloy, twin overhead-camshaft four-cylinder engine has always been the driving force which provided performance and smoothness, power and reliability, economy and flexibility, to several generations of designs which set new standards of excellence in the sporting-car market. But if engineering is to be successful, it can never be static, and while the classic Alfa engine embodied various ideas which were absolutes in terms of efficiency and utility, there were still improvements which could be made. For example, the existing engine had an excellent layout in terms of the way in which the camshafts, valves and combustion chambers were arranged in each of the cylinders. But it was still an in-line unit, and as such it suffered from one inherent drawback – the difficulty of balancing the forces produced by the different reciprocating masses as the engine turned over.

One way of solving this problem was to arrange the cylinders in two opposing banks instead of a single line: this was the so-called flat-engine configuration, used on cars which ranged from the VW Beetle to the Ferrari Boxer, and employed by Alfa themselves on the Alfasud and on the flat-twelve version of the tipo 33 sports-racing prototypes. But the main problem with flat engines was that the maximum stroke was limited in the end by the width of the car, especially where overhead camshafts were used, and the Alfasud had gone about as far as was

The heart of the larger of the current GTVs, the V6 2.5 litre fuel-injection engine, and the first large-scale production Alfa engine design for more than 30 years

Rear view of the V6, which had the traditional hemispherical combustion chambers and inclined overhead valves, but with only a single camshaft for each bank of cylinders

practical in that direction without resorting to multi-cylinder engines to produce any increase in capacity.

There was one other way of producing smoother operation and lower stresses: by arranging the cylinders in a vee, it was possible to eliminate at least some of the out-of-balance forces. Alfa had themselves produced a V8 engine in 1970 with the cylinder banks set at 90 degrees to one another, with twin overhead-camshafts per bank, 80 mm bores and 64.5 mm stroke, producing a capacity of 2593 cc, which was used to power the limited-production Alfa Montreal. This unit was in effect a scaled-down version of the three-litre V8 used in the 1969 version of the tipo 33 sports-racing car.

For a V6 engine however, setting the cylinder banks at 60 degrees to one another produces smoother and better-

The V6 version of the GTV, outwardly almost identical to the latest version of the four-cylinder car, apart from the fairing on top of the bonnet-lid

balanced running, and because of the need to take up less and less of the car's length with power unit, this offered a better way forward in the eyes of Alfa's engineers. In keeping with the most modern thinking, they sought to increase the capacity by widening the cylinder bores rather than lengthening the stroke, and in early 1979 they unveiled a new top-of-the-range saloon, using the Alfetta body and chassis, but powered by an 88 mm bore, 68.3 mm stroke 60 degree V6, 2492 cc all-alloy engine delivering 160 bhp at 5800 rpm. The valve gear followed the Alfasud pattern in having only a single overhead camshaft for each cylinder bank, though in this case the valves were still arranged in the traditional Alfa manner in two inclined rows opening into the roof of an almost hemispherical combustion

115

The interior was little changed – apart from more colourful trim. The driver's seat still had the crank handle to lift the seat up to give shorter drivers better visibility

chamber. The inlet valves were operated directly through inverted buckets, while the exhaust valves were actuated through transverse rockers.

The original version of the engine used in the Alfa Six, as the saloon was called, was fed by no less than half a dozen Solex single-choke carburettors. But when it appeared at the end of 1980 in the GTV, it was given Bosch L-Jetronic fuel injection. This version delivered the same peak power of 160 bhp, at the slightly higher speed of 6000 rpm, and though the torque was slightly lower than in the carburettored version, the lower weight of the coupé made this rather less of a drawback than it might otherwise have been.

Several alterations had to be made to the GTV to cope with the bigger engine: larger couplings were fitted to the double-section propeller shaft, and the single-plate GTV clutch was fitted with a twin-plate unit of the same diameter to fit within the same bell-housing. But tougher gears, clutch thrust bearings, transmission bearings and larger master cylinders were also fitted to cope with nearly 25 per cent extra power and 18 per cent higher torque. Other changes, though, were less easy to justify, like the use of a lower first gear ratio, though this was

Left and below *The dashboard was definitely an improvement though. Grouping both the speedometer and tachometer behind the steering wheel, together with the clock, and locating the other dials in the centre of the dash, was a much more logical arrangement (left). The front end of the new car was similar to the latest GTV 2.0s, with an extra bonnet-lid bulge – both had replaced the two-piece chin spoiler with a one-piece unit having an air-intake grille in the centre*

Careful detail design, with heavier bumpers, more spoilers and an almost total lack of chrome, make the basically unchanged bodyshape of the GTV look fresh and attractive

compensated for by a higher fifth, which pushed the top speed up to almost 130 mph. Stopping was given as much thought as going, with slightly larger ventilated discs being fitted to the front wheels, and wider 195/60 tyres on Campagnolo alloy wheels.

One more detail was changed, and not before time. The old dashboard layout was replaced at last by a more efficient and rational arrangement, with speedometer, rev-counter and clock set in three matching dials behind the steering wheel, with only the smaller subsidiary dials (fuel gauge, water temperature gauge and oil pressure gauge) remaining in the centre panel. At the same time, the dials were shrouded by a deeper dashboard moulding to cut down reflections in the screen. Externally, chrome had all but vanished, apart from the radiator shield: window surrounds, bumpers, doorhandles, headlamp surrounds and mirror housings were all now finished in matt black, and the underseal protection was toughened up considerably. Because of the greater clearances needed by the fuel-injection system, the GTV6, as the new car was designated, had a noticeable bulge in the centre of the bonnet-lid, and the old divided front spoiler was replaced by a black one-piece unit louvred in the centre to allow cooling air to reach the sump.

The GTV6 was not intended as a replacement for the existing GTV. Alfa themselves went on record as explaining that the introduction of the new model was due mainly to an increase in sports-car sales in the USA, which presumably also accounted for the replacement of carburettors by fuel injection. But apart from the changes to brakes and transmission, and the giveaway bulge in the bonnet lid, the GTV 2.0, as the original GTV was restyled, was given the same styling changes as its larger stablemate.

All of which brings us, so far as the development story is concerned, more or less up-to-date. But how do the cars stand up to today's competition, a full decade after the first Alfetta GT made its appearance? After driving a two-litre GTV, as I did for four years on an everyday basis, the extra power and flexibility of the V6 comes as a blinding revelation. More even than the turbo version of the two-litre car, *this* is what the Alfetta GT ought to have been all along. The clutch feels appreciably heavier and the power bulge on the bonnet is a reminder that this is a different proposition from the original car, but it still leaves one ill-prepared for the transformation in the car's essential character. Press the clutch, engage first gear, press the accelerator pedal and you're away, with a smooth and almost effortless acceleration in the mode of one of the larger-engined BMWs or Mercedes-Benz, let's say. But the GTV is still an Alfa, and the angry growl of the engine is a powerful and evocative sound, especially when backed up with this kind of instant response.

Yet there seems to be little price to pay, save for the inevitable increase in fuel consumption. The engine

At the rear end too, real changes were few: different rear light clusters and bigger bumpers are the main differences between the GTV6 and its original 1.8 litre predecessor

must be heavier than the four-cylinder unit, yet the steering is as light and lively as any preceding Alfa, and it makes the car a joy to handle along twisting roads, with the superbly balanced chassis making light of the most severe cornering requirements. It is a noisy car though, so enjoyment and comfort depends to a certain extent on the driver having the kind of enthusiasm which helps him to regard the busy mechanical chatter of camshafts and valve train as a delight rather than a drawback.

Certainly there is one respect in which both versions of the Alfetta GTV have proved themselves worthy successors to the Alfas of the past, and that is in the record they have built up in the toughest of international races and rallies. The original Alfetta GT started to prove its mettle as long ago as 1975, when it won the Elba Rally and the San Remo Rally, with a third place in the Tour de Corse, while in the following season the cars went on to win the second division in the European Touring Car Championship. Since then, they have notched up innumerable race and rally wins, including two more European Rally Championships, until the GTV6 was ready to take over. This has taken an

Still a striking and elegant shape after more than ten years – the 1984 version of the GTV

already splendid story several steps further – in 1982 the GTV6 won the European Touring Car Championship again, and the rally version of the car took Bruno Bentivogli to victory in Group N of the Italian Rally Championship. Finally, in 1983 (the last full year for which Alfa's detailed results figures are available at the time of writing), the GTV6 won yet another European Touring Car Championship with ten outright wins and two second places, the French Production Car Championship and the Group A International Rally Championship, again for Bruno Bentivogli, including wins in both the Group A category and the private-entrant categories in the Monte Carlo Rally.

In the end, perhaps the best way of summing up the appeal of the GTV6 in particular, and the GTV range as a whole, is to look at what objective road-testers have had to say about them, over the years. In 1975, the *Autocar* said of the original Alfetta GT that – 'the gearchange is in no way up to the standard of the older Alfas with conventionally placed gearchanges. There is a feeling of rubber remoteness about the Alfetta's change which is, perhaps not unexpected'. On the other hand, they also felt: 'Once the weight and gearing of the steering have

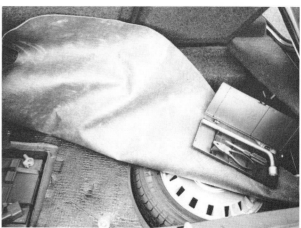

Both above *The modest bootspace is remarkably uncluttered, as bulky components like the spare wheel and the battery are set into recesses below the floor*

been accepted, one can realize where it excels, which is in the way it provides exact information from the front wheels. The driver is never in any doubt what they are trying to do, and how much of a margin they have left. This excellence of feel is one of the most appealing things about the Alfetta and goes hand in hand with roadholding of a high order. . . . The handling is as well-balanced as one would expect. It means that, within limits, the car handles according to the way it is driven. A late, clumsy entry to a corner brings understeer: a slow entry and the early application of power pushes the tail wide; and a smooth, almost racing approach is rewarded with handling as near neutral as one would wish. . . .'

Two years later, *Motor Trend* tested the American version of the car, the Sprint GT (the name Alfetta was dropped in the States when it was realized that its glorious European racing associations were largely lost on Americans). This had the 1962 cc engine, but fitted with Spica fuel injection and emission-control equipment it delivered 115 bhp peak power at 6000 rpm. They found that: 'In the case of the GT, pushing it hard provoked a balanced and controllable neutral drift. The bigger the hurry, the more the drift. It isn't something the driver does consciously as in a more traditional

sports car, but something the car does by itself, but
gently and predictably. You pick an apex, preferably a
late one, aim for it and then, as you touch it, pounce on
the throttle to the right degree and the car moves
forward and outward until it is in the proper attitude to
be straightened out and given more throttle. Very
pleasant and almost too precise. . . .'

Finally, the GTV6. *Autocar* found the gearchange
'. . . especially sticky and heavy between the lower gears,
if otherwise free and precise enough'. On the other hand,
although the driver comfort came in for criticism: '. . . the
driving position represents a bad example of the
typically Italian one, where one has no choice but to
drive with arms outstretched if one's legs are not to be

*One of the virtues of the
original Giugiaro design was
the large window area, and
for a GT coupé the interior is
uncommonly light and airy*

cramped', and Alfa were criticized for not curing the trouble by making the steering column adjustable for reach as well as for angle, they too praised the handling of the car in extravagant terms. 'Once the suspension is loaded up in corners, the GTV6 sticks to the road beautifully with little roll, and without being at all upset by mid-corner surface changes or bumps. For the most part the driver feels wonderfully in contact with the road, being able to place the car accurately, and easily sense the limit of adhesion as it approaches. In extremis, the extra power of the GTV6, improved chassis and extra grip, combine to make it a much more neutrally balanced car than the first 2-litre GTVs. . . .'

Motor for their part were eventually to refer to the GTV6 as a 'curate's egg' design. The bad parts were

Below and right *The splendid combination of a GTV and an open road (below) – a quality combined with Alfa's engineering tradition to woo GTV6 buyers (right) in this American ad*

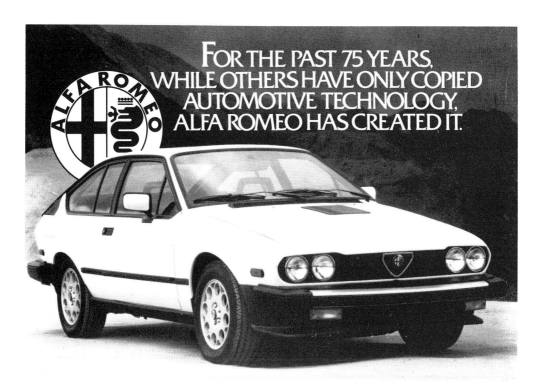

FOR THE PAST 75 YEARS, WHILE OTHERS HAVE ONLY COPIED AUTOMOTIVE TECHNOLOGY, ALFA ROMEO HAS CREATED IT.

For the past 75 years, Alfa Romeo has been single-mindedly pursuing only one goal: The passionate engineering of high performance automobiles for sophisticated drivers.

It has been this philosophy of engineering excellence that has kept Alfa Romeo consis-

tently in the forefront of automotive technology. As a result, we have pioneered some of the most outstanding technical achievements in automotive history. Like dual overhead cams as far back as 1914. 4-wheel disc brakes as

standard equipment on our production cars for the past 20 years. Fuel injection as early as 1968.

The variable-valve-timing system on our classic Spider Veloce was born on a Formula 1 racer. And the DeDion suspension system on our high-performance GTV-6 can only be found on one other automobile: a $120,000 Aston Martin. What's more, the 1985 Alfa Romeos start at only $13,495.* And all carry a 3 year/ 36,000 mile warranty.**

However, what continues to propel Alfa Romeo into the future is not solely an uncompromising passion for engineering. It's our unwavering enthusiasm for the excitement of driving.

THE MOST PASSIONATELY ENGINEERED CARS IN THE WORLD.

Alfa Romeo

The GTV6 has built up an increasingly successful competiton record – and Alfa publicity has made the most of it . . .

ALFA ROMEO WINS AGAIN & AGAIN & AGAIN

Performance from the 2.5 litre 160bhp V6 engine with electronic fuel injection.

Roadholding from the finely balanced GTV6 chassis with the De Dion rear axle.

The Alfa Romeo GTV6 adds up to a real competitive opportunity.

Congratulations from Alfa Romeo to the teams who took their opportunity and won.

Manufacturers' Award. European Saloon Car Championship

Norris Miles. Drivers and Manufacturers'Award. UniRoyal Production Saloon Car Championship;

Jon Dooley. Winner - Class B. Trimoco RAC British Saloon Car Championship.

Photographs by LAT Photographic.

Alfa Romeo
The Art of Technology

Alfetta GTV6 racing has been exciting around the world but no more so than in Britain where Jon Dooley (car no. 30) has been battling with the Terry Drury Racing team cars (car no. 41 driven by Paul Smith) in the national saloon car racing championship. Successful they certainly are

highlighted as the gearchange '. . . earned loud raspberries from all our testers, one of whom found it so baulky, clonky and imprecise that he thought the linkage was in the process of disintegrating . . .' and an awkward clutch action '. . . which requires a long movement to disengage fully, and yet takes up the drive again only at the very top of its travel', and the car was finally assessed as a mixture of 'great looks with an ill-planned interior; a glorious engine with flawed chassis and transmission. There's nothing fundamentally wrong with the Alfa's layout on paper, and it shouldn't take much to get it right, despite a series of minor revamps which have so far failed to take up the challenge'.

Harsh words indeed, and to be frank they scarcely meet the reality of driving today's GTV6 in earnest. Yes, the gearchange is slower, and heavier than the Alfas of old, but yes the engine is magnificent, smooth and powerful and just noisy enough to set the blood racing when accelerating hard down an empty road. Yes, the driving position is far better suited to shorter drivers than it is to tall ones, and the roof comes too close for comfort. But yes the car handles beautifully, letting the driver decide the handling characteristics he wants, to suit the corner, the surface and his own technique.

Perhaps *What Car?* came closest to the truth, when they said of the GTV6 that 'the mixture is marred for the sporting driver by the hit-or-miss gearchange, the woeful lack of headroom, the poor dashboard and dismal ventilation, and the feeling of chassis flexing when cornering hard'. But they also said: 'The GTV6 so very nearly makes it as the all-time classic grand tourer: the Alfa name is legend, the 2+2 coupé body's styling fabulous and the injection V6 magnificent, combining superb flexibility, power and smoothness with an evocative race-track six-cylinder howl. The ride comfort is good too, and the 25 mpg fuel economy highly competitive . . . a few minor changes would make it the most enjoyable of all'. To any Alfa enthusiast, these words are at once saddening, yet heartening. With the GTV story not yet over, can we still hope that having achieved so much with these cars, Alfa will still have time to make those changes and earn the design the place it surely deserves?

Specifications

Model	length	width	height	weight (lb)	first	second	third	fourth	fifth	r/axle ratio
							gear ratios			
Alfetta GT	13′ 9″	5′ 5″	4′ 4″	2393	3.30	2.00	1.37	1.04	0.83	4.10
Alfetta GT 1.6	13′ 9″	5′ 5″	4′ 4″	2423	3.30	2.00	1.37	1.04	0.83	4.30
Alfetta 2000GTV	13′ 9″	5′ 5″	4′ 4″	2423	3.30	1.956	1.345	1.026	0.83	4.10
Alfetta GTV Turbo	13′ 9″	5′ 5″	4′ 4″	2475	3.30	2.00	1.37	1.04	0.83	4.10
Alfetta GTV6	14′ 0″	5′ 5″	4′ 4″	2610	3.50	1.956	1.345	1.026	0.78	4.10

Engine details

Model	no. of cyls	bore (mm)	stroke (mm)	capacity (cc)	carburation	valve gear	maximum power	maximum torque
Alfetta GT	four	80	88.5	1779	two twin-choke Dell'Orto carbs	twin overhead camshafts	122 bhp @ 5500 rpm	123 lb.ft @ 4400 rpm
Alfetta GT 1.6	four	78	82	1567	two twin-choke Dell'Orto carbs	twin overhead camshafts	109 bhp @ 5600 rpm	
Alfetta 2000GTV	four	84	88.5	1962	two twin-choke Dell'Orto carbs	twin overhead camshafts	130 bhp @ 5400 rpm	132 lb.ft @ 4000 rpm

Alfetta GTV Turbo	four	84	88.5	1962	Garrett AiResearch turbo-charger – two Dell'Orto twin-choke carburettors	twin overhead camshafts	175 bhp @ 5500 rpm	190 lb.ft @ 4000 rpm
Alfetta GTV6	vee-six	88	68.3	2492	Bosch L-Jetronic fuel injection	single overhead camshaft per cylinder bank with push-rod operated exhaust valves	160 bhp @ 5600 rpm	157 lb.ft @ 4000 rpm

Performance figures

Model	acceleration times (sec)								top speed (mph)
	0–30	0–40	0–50	0–60	0–70	0–80	0–90	0–100	
Alfetta GT	3.0	4.3	6.7	9.4	12.9	17.3	23.4	32.2	117
Alfetta GT 1.6	4.0	6.1	8.8	12.1	16.5				110
Alfetta 2000GTV	2.9	4.1	6.2	8.9	12.2	16.1	21.7	29.3	118
Alfetta GTV Turbo	2.8	3.7	5.6	8.1	11.0	14.1	17.8	22.0	124
Alfetta GTV6	2.8	4.5	6.3	8.8	11.7	14.7	19.4	24.3	130

Model		speeds in gears (mph)					fuel consumption (mpg)			
	first	second	third	fourth	fifth		average	touring	hard driving	steady 70 mph
Alfetta GT	31	52	76	100	117		26.1	30.8	21.6	33.3
Alfetta GT 1.6	30	50	73	96	110		26.7	31.2	20.4	34.1
Alfetta 2000GTV	31	52	76	100	118		25.6	30.3	21.0	28.9
Alfetta GTV Turbo	33	52	76	100	124		22.3	26.7	17.8	28.4
Alfetta GTV6	31	56	81	107	130		25.2	30.4	20.6	29.2

Production figures

Alfetta GT
1974: 6440 units; 1975: 11,974 units; 1976: 3533 units.
Total: 21,947 units.

Alfetta GT 1.6
1976: 4262 units; 1977: 7935 units; 1978: 3321 units; 1979: 787 units; 1980: 618 units.
Total: 16,923 units.

Alfetta 2000GTV
1975: 1942 units; 1976: 14,254 units; 1977: 14,801 units; 1978: 12,757 units; 1979: 9289 units;
1980: 6313 units; 1981: 2955 units; 1982: 5308 units; 1983: 4150 units.
Total (to end 1983–1984 figures not yet available): 72,039 units

Alfetta GTV6
1979: 2 units; 1980: 1179 units; 1981: 5805 units; 1982: 4735 units; 1983: 4118 units.
Total (to end 1983–1984 figures not yet available): 15,839 units.

Acknowledgements

Sincere thanks to everyone involved in the making of this book and in particular to the following who supplied the photographs:

Barry Needham of Alfa Romeo (GB); Mirco Decet; Tim Parker Collection; David Owen; London Art Technical (the photographic service to *Motor Sport* magazine); Bell & Colvill Ltd and finally the Alfa Romeo factory in Milan who contributed greatly.

Index